How to Get Over
Global Mental Health Crisis
Caused by COVID-19 Pandemic

See
the Door
Opened

Andrew Yoo, Ph.D.

ISBN: 9798655850514

This book is dedicated to everyone who values themselves and tries to achieve their dreams based on their unique talent, who wants to find happiness in their present life and live in abundance, and who knows and practices that we should go together in sharing for others. You are so unique and excellent!

CONTENTS

SEE THE DOOR OPENED

ACKNOWLEDGMENTS

I would like to thank the following people for inspiring and providing me with resources to write this book:

Aberjhani	Jennifer Brown
Albert Einstein	Jessamyn West
Alexander Graham Bell	Jesus Christ
Alison Stormwolf	John Muir
Anne Wilson Schaef	Leo Buscaglia
B.K.S. Iyengar	Mahatma Gandhi
Barbara Hall	Melody Beattie
Ben Vereen	Mother Teresa
Bob Hope	Pandora Poikilos
Bobbe Somme	Patricia Neal
Buddha	Peter Shpherd
Carlos Santana	Phyllis McGinley
Dale Carnegie	Richard Bandler
Desmond Tutu	Richelle E. Goodrich

Dr. Weir Mitchell MD

Fyodor Dostoevsky

George Bernard Shaw

Haruki Murakami

Henry David Thoreau

Henry Ford

Herbert M. Shelton

Hippocrates

Hubert H. Humphrey

Humboldt

J. J. Goldwag

Jack Canfield

James Freeman Clarke

Jana Stanfield

Ricky Skaggs

Robert Dilts

Robert James Waller

SaengJin Lee

Sai Baba

Sama Guang

Sarah Fielding

Shakti Gawain

Thomas Dewar

Tori Amos

Wynton Marsalis

Wallace Huey

Yehuda Berg

YoungTaek Kim

Our mind is a small universe where all kinds of phenomena occur from time to time. Mindfulness is a shortcut to the stability and peace of the small universe.

Introduction

Human Beings become great by their deeds

Chanakya who was an ancient Indian teacher, philosopher, economist, jurist, and the royal advisor said, "A man is great by deeds, not by birth." We are noticing and learning that his words is the right and deepen philosophy through COVID-19 Pandemic. Even though 3000 years have passed, he teaches us how people should do in a global mental health crisis.

On 13 MAY 2020, the United Nations has published a report that "Policy Brief: COVID-19 and the Need for Action on Mental Health." According to the EXECUTIVE SUMMARY of the document, it is the mental health and wellbeing of whole societies that have been severely impacted by the COVID-19 crisis and are a priority to be addressed urgently.

Although the COVID-19 crisis is, in the first instance, a physical health crisis, it has the seeds of a major mental health crisis as well, if action is not taken. Good mental health is critical to the functioning of society at the best of times. It must be front and centre of every country's response to and recovery from the COVID-19 pandemic.chapter one text here. Insert chapter one text here. Insert chapter one text here. Insert chapter one text here. Insert chapter one text here. Insert chapter one text here.

What shall we do to protect ourselves from a physical health crisis and a mental health crisis as well?

Irad Eichler who is founder of Shekulo Tov suggested a few practical tips on strengthening your support system from an article "5 tips for supporting mental health during COVID-19," as follows; 1)Find and spend time with like-minded people, 2)Real-time connection is important, 3)Emotional support experts are key to designing impactful group support, 4)Share one feeling a day, and 5)Ask one person a day how they feel.

(https://www.weforum.org/agenda/2020/05/mental-healthcare-revolution-post-covid19)

As Chanakya said, we could meet many great people through their deeds in a global crisis of COVID-19 Pandemic.

On the other hand, many people still cannot be great people due to the deeds they do. Even so, everyone can be a great person through the deeds he/she does.

Above all, it is you that will be a great person. For you are a unique person in the world.

I suggest 52 short healing and recovery tips for the mind and body. For many years, I have written a short article about healing and recovery for the body and mind. The short articles were originally for me.

I had a hard time in my life for years. My efforts to overcome bad situations in business were far from success repeatedly. I wanted to stop everything. Then I met a pastor for counsel. He gave me a piece of good advice and I felt comfort and recovery hope. Thanks to his comfort and encouragement, I am here now.

At that time, the only way I could do to endure the difficulties was praying and reading the Bible and many good books or writing a short article for mindfulness. I have chosen 52 short articles from which I wrote. It will be helpful for you to read one article per week and think about your life.

I hope this book is an opportunity and a method that you can get over this crisis caused by COVID-19 Pandemic.

1 OPEN YOUR HEART, AND YOU WILL GET BETTER

What happens when people open their hearts?
They get better.

Haruki Murakami
Author of *Norwegian Wood*

The 52 images in the body of this book used the stock image of MS Office.

When you keep your heart wide open, your body and mind will be getting well. Keep your heart wide open right now for yourself and others around you. As Thomas Dewar said, minds are like parachutes… they only function when open.

2 CHERISH YOUR FRIENDS AND LOVE YOURSELF AND OTHERS

The greatest healing therapy is friendship and love.

Hubert H. Humphrey
38th Vice President of the United States

Love and friendship are unique cure-alls. For love is the fundamental principle of human relations and friendship is exposed inside the story feeling much relieved. Love yourself and others. Keep contacting your inner mind and with friends more frequently.

3 HOLD YOUR ORIGINALITY
IN HIGH REGARD

Having a low opinion of yourself is not "modesty".
It's self-destruction.
Holding your uniqueness in high regard is not "egotism".
It's a necessary precondition to happiness and success.

Bobbe Somme
Psychologist and author

How do you define yourself? How to estimate yourself has a big impact on your happiness and success.

It is common that to have a low opinion of yourself is virtue and modesty.
Of course, sometimes it's true. However, from time to time it destroys yourself. It is necessary for you to show deep respect for your uniqueness. Love and respect yourself just the way you are, for the way you are will be your originality.

To love and respect yourself is the basic element of happiness and success. Take time in a quiet place and take care of yourself about what is your uniqueness again. And have great regard for your originality.

4 DON'T MISS THE RIGHT TIME TO HEAL YOUR BODY AND MIND

Just like there's always time for pain, there's always time for healing.

Jennifer Brown
American writer

There is a proper time for everything. To study, to make money, or to pursuit to power, all need in good time. To keep your body and mind healthy, above all, you should know there is in a good time. Don't miss the right time to heal your body and mind.

5 BE CAREFUL OF YOUR CHOICE AND DON'T OBSESS OVER THE RESULTS TOO MUCH

You are free to choose your own way of life,
but you are not free to choose the results.

Herbert M. Shelton
American author

Every moment of your life is a continuous choice. You choose a priority of the day when you get up in the morning. However, some people get a good result after work of the day, others don't.

When you realize that it is free to choose the process, but not the results, you feel like a rag in body and mind. In such a case, you should encourage yourself. Nothing is worth taking care of yourself in the world.

Be careful of every choice you make in your life and don't obsess over the results too much.

6 EXPRESS YOUR GRATITUDE FOR EVEN EVERY SLIGHTEST THING AROUND YOU

Gratitude is medicine for a heart devastated by tragedy.
If you can only be thankful for the blue sky, then do so.

Richelle E. Goodrich
American author

There is always something to be thankful for being tied up in knots. When you are placed in a difficult situation, look around and express your thanks if you find anything to be thankful. Then your sorrow is decreasing, and your broken heart can heal quickly.

Thank anything that is to be thankful at this moment. An expression of gratitude is medicine for the heart.

Now I will express my thanks. I thank that I am breathing. I thank that I can write this book. Thank you for your reading it. I thank you, the readers. Thank you!

7 HEAL YOURSELF AND YOUR FAMILY BEFORE HELPING THE WORLD TO HEAL

The way you help heal the world is you start with your own family.

Mother Teresa
Roman Catholic saint

Sama Guang, the Chinese scholar, once said that "When one´s home is happy and harmonious, all goes well." It means that "Things in life begin family life." Yes, it is true. Before straightening out the world, the first thing to do is to bring the family to right. So are voluntary service and love.

For love, to love yourself is the first thing you should do. And then when you are to do voluntary service, you should start with your family and the neighborhood. To heal yourself and your family first are the best way to help   heal   the   world.

8 LOVE EVERYBODY
AS THEY ARE

Love one another and help others to rise to the higher levels,
simply by pouring out love.
Love is infectious and the greatest healing energy.

Sai Baba
Indian saint

Love is to see and accept yourself just who you are and others who they are. Love is to be proud of yourself just the way you are. Love is to respect others just the way they are. Love yourself and others.

Love is to give first without expecting anything in return. Love has strong power both changing impossible to possible and recovering those exhausted persons who are worn out in body and mind.

Love is a powerful energy for healing. The best healing energy is love. Love everybody as they are if you want to get powerful healing.

9 KEEP YOUR MIND AT PEACE FOR TRUE HEALING

Of one thing I am certain, the body is not the measure of healing,
peace is the measure.

Phyllis McGinley
American poet and author

24

If you feel something wrong with you, the target you should heal is both your body and mind. In the true sense of the word, healing your mind is more important than your body. In many cases, peace in your mind might bring healing the hurt more quickly. The reason is everything arises from your mind. True healing can happen when peace is in your mind.

10 LISTEN TO GOOD MUSIC TO GET OVER YOUR TROUBLES

Music is such a great healing balm and a great way to forget your troubles.

Ricky Skaggs
American singer

26

A piece of good music can make your soul clear. It may cure the illness in your body. It can heal your mind, too. Of course, some of the troubles that distress you also might be all forgotten from it. I bet a piece of good music shall be a healing balm for you to care for your body and mind. Music is a great healing balm.

11 SPEAK KIND WORDS, AND YOU CAN HEAL AND LIFT UP A BROKENHEARTED PERSON

The words of kindness are more healing to a drooping heart than balm or honey.

Sarah Fielding
English author

The greatest way to heal and lift the brokenhearted is to speak kind words.

There is a saying, "A good tongue is a good weapon." It emphasizes the importance of words between work and human relations. Words play a huge role in healing your body and mind.

More than anything else, kind words that you have heard are the most valuable therapeutic agent when you are totally exhausted.

Be a person who conveys an inspiring message and words of love. A broken heart can be healed by kind words.

12 LIVE THE PRESENT MOMENT MORE WISELY AND EARNESTLY

The secret of health for both mind and body is not to mourn for the past,
not to worry about the future, or not to anticipate troubles,
but to live the present moment wisely and earnestly.

Buddha

The present look of yourself is the trace of your past whether you wanted or not. You don't need to regret the past though. You cannot change the past. It is all water under the bridge now.

Certain disease can cause to look to the past. Never mind the future in advance. Don't expect when things go wrong. See your bright future and expect a positive self. When you think about your future, nothing is more important than the present. Accept yourself where you are, what you are, and what you have.

What you should do in every condition is to live your reality now wiser and more earnestly than ever before. Your body and mind are one. To keep your body and mind healthy, it is necessary for you to exhibit the wisdom of living present. The secret of health is to live the present moment wisely and earnestly.

13 BE A PERSON WITH A STRONG POSITIVE ATTITUDE

A strong positive attitude will create more miracles than any wonder drug.

Patricia Neal
American actress

No matter how good medicine you give to a patient who does not have a positive attitude, it does not work. Because a strong positive attitude is the root of the miracles.

If you want to become a person who experiences a miracle in daily life, have a strong positive attitude. The stronger positive attitude you have, the bigger miracle you can make.

14 KEEP YOUR BODY AND MIND HEALTHY

It is health that is real wealth and not pieces of gold and silver.

Mahatma Gandhi
Indian Independence Movement, Nonviolent resistance

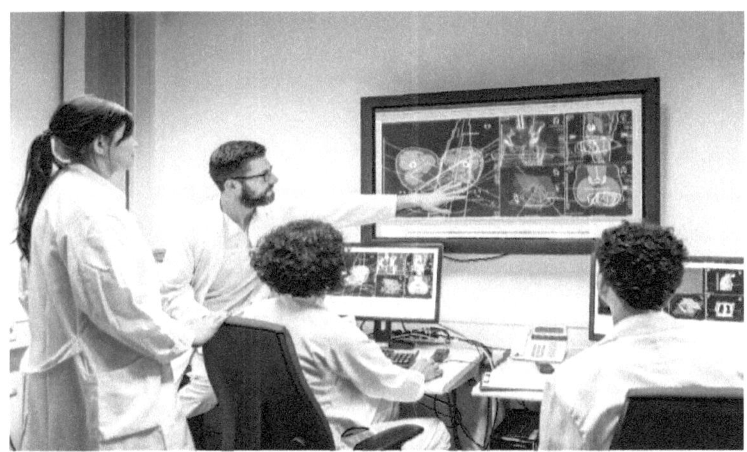

There is much wealth to enrich the world and people's lives. The more gold and silver treasure you have, the better your quality of life becomes. However, if a person who is not healthy has a lot of money, and if one cannot recover one's health with money, the value of money decreases. Money is only a white elephant.

The real wealth you should have is health. The real wealth is to keep your body and mind healthy.

15 BE CAREFUL TO LISTEN TO YOUR BODY SIGNALS

Our bodies communicate to us clearly and specifically
if we are willing to listen.

Shakti Gawain
An author in the field of personal development

Your body sends a lot of signals to you without stopping. However, you are sometimes ignoring or missing the signals. To recognize signals that your body sends to you, you are only willing to listen to them. When you are willing to listen to your body's signals, then you can hear their message.

Your body is always trying to communicate with you. If you are willing to listen to your body's signals, you can hear them clear and specific. Most diseases can be cured if you can recognize the signal at the very beginning when your body sends to you.

16 ASK FOR HELP
FROM THE HEALING FORCE WITHIN YOU
BEFORE GOING TO SEE A DOCTOR

Everyone has a doctor in him or her; we just have to help it in its work.
The natural healing force within each one of us is the greatest force in getting well.

Hippocrates
Greek physician

You already have all the resources you need. That is, you have already all the answers to the problem in you. You only cannot find the solution. That is why you ask doctors or medicine to cure your physical disease and you ask counselors or coaches to heal the illness of the mind. Despite that, you should find out the solution to a radical cure or healing in you.

As the old sayings say, every variety of bodily ill or illness of the mind originates in the mind, the mind is significant. Have a good and funny day with your peace of mind.

17 CHEER UP AND EXPECT YOU TO BE WELL

Never hurry. Take plenty of exercise.
Always be cheerful. Take all the sleep you need.
Expect to be well.

James Freeman Clarke
American theologian and author

Thank the beginning of the day when you wake up in the morning. For it starts the new history of your life. Never hurry up whatever may happen or under any circumstances. Take time for exercise.

Though life itself is not always funny or pleasant, enjoy yourself as far as possible. Your mind affects your physical health. Getting enough sleep is the great secret of keeping you healthy. Get enough sleep every night.

And expect to be well. Pretend to get better every moment. Positive imagination serves to your servant to optimize a given opportunity. Your brain cannot distinguish imagination from reality. It has a habit of achieving that you can imagine. Be cheerful and expect to be well. Your thoughts change your feeling into good or bad. They also affect your body.

18 BELIEVE IN YOUR MIND POWER

All healing Starts in the mind.

Alison Stormwolf
Scottish poet and healer

42

There is an old saying that everything depends on the mind. It means that all things are made by the mind. It is also said that every variety of bodily ill or illness of the mind originates from in the mind. It is the same that all healing starts from in the mind.

To have a peaceful mind starts to heal body and mind, and soul. Believe in your mind power when you heal disorder in your body and mind Look up in the sky once a day. And yell, "I am healthy and well."

19 DO YOUR MIND'S ACTIVITIES CONSTANTLY AND PHYSICAL EXERCISE REGULARLY

True enjoyment comes from activity of the mind and exercise of the body;
the two are ever united.

Humboldt
Prussian polymath

Where do you think come from true enjoyment? From time to time it comes from the mind and movement of the body. However, you can enjoy yourself to the fullest when your body and mind are united. Because your body and mind are one system, not separated. True enjoyment comes from activity of the mind and exercise of the body

20 HEAD UP AND LAUGH AT THE SKY
WHEN YOU STAND SEVERE PAIN OR SADNESS

I have seen what a laugh can do.
It can transform almost unbearable tears into something bearable, even hopeful.

Bob Hope
American-British comedian

It is said that a laugh can cure every kind of illness. However, it is subject to change with time and place. You are to be blamed when you laugh at an off-key situation. If you face a serious difficulty, it is natural that tears flow. When you overcome in that situation, laugh can transform the difficulty into a great power to endure it. From time to time smile will add up strong positive energy.

There are times that tears are running down like running water. At that time, head up to the sky. And smile. Then you shall have a strange power to stand the difficult situation. And the power will change your tears into hope. A laugh can transform tears into hope.

21 RESPECT AND TREAT YOURSELF AS A WORTHWHILE PERSON

Learn to deal with the fact that you are not a perfect person,
but you are a person that deserves respect and honesty.

Pandora Poikilos
Author of Excuse Me, My Brains Have Stepped Out

No one is perfect. Nevertheless, everyone is a worthwhile person to respect, for his/her presence itself is vastly important. It is impossible for you to be perfect, but it is necessary that you should be honest.

Many people are troubled with the fixed idea that people must perfect when they do business. It becomes the cause of ruin in their body and mind. You are only a man of common clay, not God. You had better get out of aiming at perfection.

You are being itself is a worthwhile person to be respected. Give a shout, "I am a worthwhile person."

22 IMAGINE CONSTANTLY WITH YOUR INFINITE POTENTIAL

The power of imagination makes us infinite.

John Muir
Scottish American naturalist, author, environmental philosopher

Imagination expands your possibilities and leads you into the bigger world. Everything has come true if you can imagine. Imagination demolishes the limitation of your thoughts and opens infinite possibilities. Imagination leads you into the bigger world

Imagine! Experience the world of infinite possibilities. The world is a big place. And there are many things waiting to be explored.

23 MIND YOUR P'S AND Q'S

Gracious words are a honeycomb,
sweet to the soul and healing to the bones.

Proverbs 16:24

There is an old saying in Korea, "A soft answer turns away wrath." And there is also an old saying, "The pen is the mightier than the swords." These emphasize the importance of the words. There are lots of books cover a subject about words and speech. It means you need to mind your P's and Q's. Gracious words can heal the body and mind.

An expert said that our brain cannot recognize negative words. Using positive words is more important than any other thing. Positive words give positive effects on your brain. If your input is positive words, the output is also positive results. Positive words can rescue the soul and cure physical diseases.

The bottom line is that you must be careful about how you behave or you should remember to be polite.

*

24 LIVE YOUR LIFE AS THOUGH EVERYTHING IS A MIRACLE

There are only two ways to live your life.
One is as though nothing is a miracle.
The other is as though everything is a miracle.

Albert Einstein
Theoretical physicist

Your life is like a miracle. Everything is a miracle such as what you were born, what you can think, what you can talk about, what you can see, and what you eat. As Albert Einstein said, to live your life in two ways; to live as though nothing is a miracle or to live as though everything is a miracle. It is up to you what life do you live.

What do you think about living as though everything is a miracle?

Melody Beattie says that "Live your life from your heart. Share from your heart. And your story will touch and heal people's souls." You can heal others' souls. It is not the work of experts or specialists to heal people's souls. You only have to live your life and share it. Then it will move and touch the others' minds and cure the others' souls.

To live your life that arises spontaneously within your heart and share your own goodwill generously will write your story. And people will be moved and can be cured from reading or hearing it. You can heal the others' souls, too.

25 TO TREAT ILLNESS, CONTROL YOUR MIND AND TAKE MEDICINE

Medicine is only palliative.
For behind disease lies the cause and this cause NO DRUG can reach.

Dr. Weir Mitchell MD
American physician, scientist, novelist, and poet

To treat physical illness, you should take medicine first. Every disease has the cause of disease and in many cases, it starts with a mind. You can treat physical disease with a drug. Mind, however, cannot be treated any medicine. It is the best way to control the mind in various ways.

Such various ways as to love, thank, compliment, forgive, consider, pray, laugh, meditate, say positive words is a good way to control your mind. Choose one or two and practice. It is the most important thing you should do

26 NEVER FIND OUT OTHERS' FAULTS

Don't find fault. Find a remedy.

Henry Ford
American industrialist

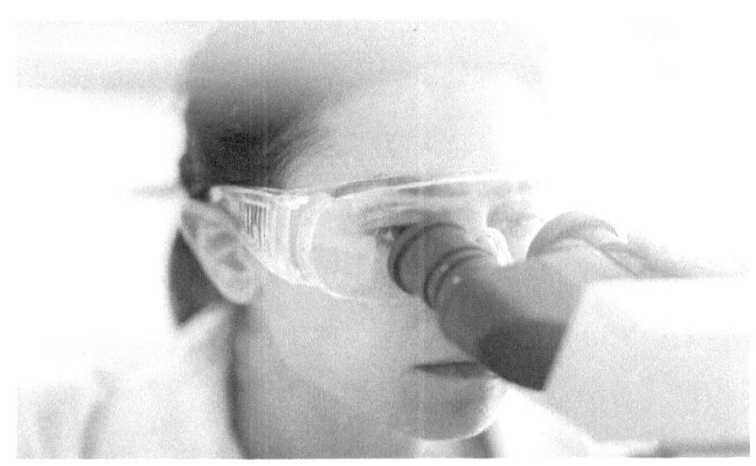

Many people often tend to find out others' mistakes or faults in their human relations or on business transactions. An old saying, "The pot calls the kettle black" is truly descriptive of selfishness or Egocentric Bias of human beings. No one has his/her faults, though. Everybody makes mistakes. Before looking for the others' fault, people should look around to acknowledge his/her own imperfections.

When you find out someone in distress, you had better help those who are in trouble. Then our society becomes a community in peace and prosperity. Let's save our society. Your loving and caring character which gives others will return at some future day.

27 SHARE YOUR STORY TO HEAL YOURSELF

I love sharing my story. It's endlessly healing.

Ben Vereen
American actor

Do you have any hidden stories within yourself? Are you depressed in spirit so that a hidden story lodged in your mind?

If so, unfold your mind. Tell your hidden story to a credible person. After you unfold the mind, you will be light-hearted. At last, you shall have peace of mind.

Sharing your story is to heal yourself.

28 CARRY JOY
IN YOUR MIND

Where humanity sowed faith, hope, and unity, joy's garden blossomed.

Aberjhani
A historian, columnist, and editor

The humanity that loves people itself is very important. And if love gives people to trust, hope, and achieve harmony, there must be a joyful place(garden) and everyone will be all smile.

Love sows the seeds of trust, hope, and harmony in your mind. Then the seeds grow and make the joyful garden in your mind. As a result, the garden is becoming in bloom fully. Bloom in the joy's garden in your mind.

As Carlos Santana said, "If you carry joy in your heart, you can heal any moment." Your life is not always in the state of perfect joy and sorrow. There is a time for joy or sorrow from time to time. However, you should always carry joy irrespective of circumstance. If you have carried joy in the heart, you can bring out the joy. Joy is strong energy for healing.

29 DO ALL THE GOOD THAT YOU CAN DO

I cannot do all the good that the world needs,
but the world needs all the good that I can do.

Jana Stanfield
Speaker, songwriter and recording artist

We greet the New Year once a year. Every time welcoming the new year, we look forward to and wish for a happy new year. Although it seems like the same sun rises every day, we call it the New Year once a year. And we hope many things in the new year.

We have a hard time trying to do what the world needs, what other people around us need. Put down the mind that you should satisfy everyone. Instead of that, please do even a small thing for the good things you can do. For all those small good things are what the world needs.

30 SAY LIFE-SAVING WORDS

A broken bone can heal, but the wound a word opens can fester forever.

Jessamyn West
American librarian

It is easy to cure physical injury in daily life. But it is not easy to heal the broken heart caused by the words between people. It may leave a trace in the heart. So, we should say life-saving words. For example, the tradition sharing well-wishing remarks on New Year's Day is the wisdom of life, which should inherit and develop.

Say a good word right now to the people around you. Say a word that saves a soul. Say a word that gives hope. A good word will save people. A good word will raise a person.

31 TO HEAL YOUR MIND,
GET OUT OF YOUR OWN WAY

There are so many ways to heal.
Arrogance may have a place in technology, but not in healing.
I need to get out of my own way if I am to heal.

Anne Wilson Schaef
American clinical psychologist

There are so many ways to cure your physical illness and to heal your mind. An arrogant manner, which is called pride, is a significant part if you want to improve scientific technology. However, it is not helpful for you to cure physical illness and to heal the mind. Especially, it is far from for healing your mind. It needs to be careful to listen to others' opinions and to get out of being stubborn.

The wider the range of your choice is, the more chance you might be healed.

32 SEIZE THE RIGHT TIME AND OPPORTUNITY FOR HEALING

Healing is a matter of time,
but it is sometimes also a matter of opportunity.

Hippocrates
Greek physician

Hippocrates, who is called the father of medicine, said that though time is an important thing to heal, from time to time opportunity is also important. That means although there is a right time to heal or cure, it is also important to seize a chance to meet a suitable person or circumstances.

It is said that physical disease become known to everybody is a good way to cure. It is simply a matter of time and opportunity. When you reveal your disease to everyone, you can seize the chance to cure or heal at the right time and appropriate method.

As the words, "Time heals all wounds.", though time heals the matter of mind, it is necessary to meet an expert in the field. A way to heal is different from person to person. It is not easy to know the right time, but a matter of time is the first thing to heal.

The root of healing is to a matter of time what the completion of healing is to a matter of opportunity. Time and opportunity are given to everybody, but it is rare to grab them for his/her own. Seize the right time and opportunity if you have any trouble. It is up to you what you will choose.

33 SPEND A LOT OF TIME WITH CHILDREN

The soul is healed by being with children.

Fyodor Dostoevsky
Russian novelist

Children's mind is pure. On the other hand, the grown-ups' mind is very complicated. Of course, adults also were once a pure child. But as time goes on, pure children are gradually changed complicated by going through the hardships of life. That is why a complicated man can recover the pure mind if he/she lives with pure children.

When adults have much time with children, they can return to the state of the pure soul. If you(adults) don't have much time to play or to live with the children, remember and recall when you were a child.

Watch the time with your eyes, listen to with your ears, and feel with your body when you were a pure child. When you look back on your childhood, your tired souls might be healed and become pure again.

34 BE BRAVE
FOR HEALING

Healing takes courage, and we all have courage,
even if we have to dig a little to find it.

Tori Amos
American singer-songwriter

To heal the body and mind takes courage. Taking courage is especially required when you need to heal the mind. It serves as momentum to lift your life a step further.

You should go to the doctor's if you discover physical symptoms coming to the surface. If you ignore the symptom, others can become aware of them. On the other hand, the symptom of your mind cannot reveal to the surface. So, it is necessary for you to take courage. Be brave!

When you sense any strange symptom in your mind, then ask a piece of advice to others. After you open your mind to somebody, your mind can recover the normal mentality. Take courage. Healing starts from when you are taking courage.

35 DO SOMETHING DIFFERENT IF YOU WOULD LIKE TO BE DIFFERENT

If you want to be different, do something different.

Wynton Marsalis
American trumpeter

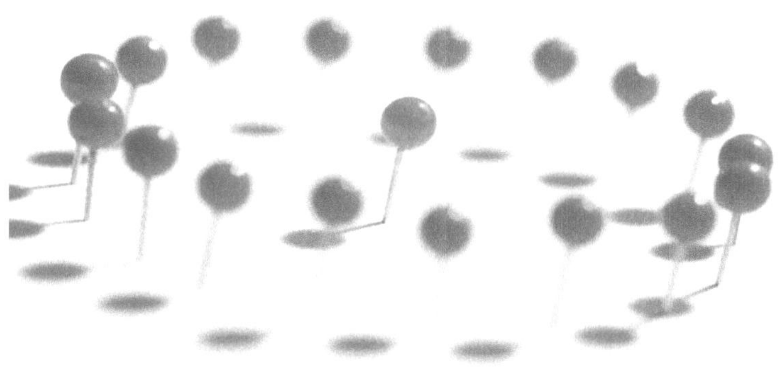

Most of the people make it a regular rule to make a new resolution each time when a day, a week, a month, or a year has newly begun. You might expect many things from renewing the resolution, but it's very difficult for you to change the habitual action.

Action should be different when your hope is to be different. If a goal is setting, there must be various ways to get to the goal. When you give something to try, but the results are not satisfied, try again and again until you are satisfied. There are many ways that you are going to try and get to the goal.

Do you want to be different? If so, do something different. Then you will get as you expect and hope.

36 TO REMEDY FOR LOVE, LOVE MORE

There is no remedy for love but to love more.

Henry David Thoreau
American essayist, poet, and philosopher

Are you hurt for love? Have you ever cried for love? If you ever so, have you done remedy after being hurt or crying? Some people say that "Love is to give unconditionally." If you have felt hurt or sad for love, the love may be conditional love. It is said that "Only love can remedy for love." Love only. Only love.

Why don't you love more than ever before?

37 HAVE COMPASSION FOR A PERSON WHO IS SORROWFUL OR WOUNDED

Our sorrows and wounds are healed only when we touch them with compassion.

Buddha

Life is a succession of a joyful occasion and a sorrowful matter. Sometimes you might be encouraged or hurt and discouraged by your relationship with the people around you. However, it restricts enjoying an opulent lifestyle to live with sorrow and hurt that we have.

To live and enjoy a bountiful life, it is necessary to heal the sorrow and hurt. It is very important to accept and admit because of the sorrow and hurt that we have are also a part of our lives. Sorrow and hurt can be cured or healed by watching for and touching with compassion.

38 PUT ANGER, HURT, OR PAIN OUT OF YOUR MIND

Don't hold to anger, hurt, or pain.
They steal your energy and keep you from love.

Leo Buscaglia
American author and motivational speaker

As happiness and joy are a part of your life, so are anger, hurt, or pain. But they decrease the energy from your lives and make you think negatively. They also interrupt to spring up the loving thought. Though they are a part of your lives, you must stop holding them because you should spring up the loving thought and produce a result.

Take a load off your mind. Anger, hurt, or pain takes positive energy away from you. They deprive you of the power of love. Get away from the negative feeling. Be free of the negative feeling.

On the other hand, you had better hold on the feeling of happiness and joy that spring up the loving and produce a result. Remember that happiness keeps making choices for yourself moment to moment. Accept the feeling of love, thank, consideration, and forgiveness.

The positive feeling can cause better results than negative feelings. However, even a little negative feeling deprives you of the power of good energy. Leading a rich life without anger, hurt or pain is a matter of your choice.

What do you choose?

39 UTILIZE AND STRENGTHEN A RECOVERING METHOD YOUR HEART HAS FOR ITSELF

The human heart has a way of making itself large again
even after it's been broken into a million pieces.

Robert James Waller
American author

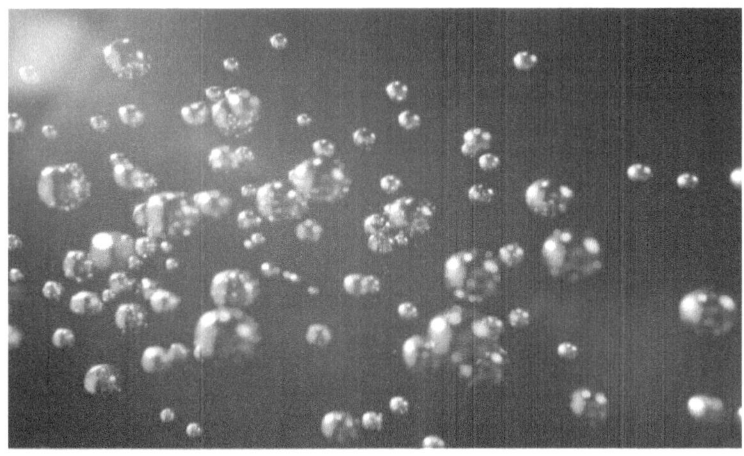

People sometimes say that "Physical disease can be cured, but the scar of the heart can't be healed." On the other hand, Robert James Waller said, "The human heart has a way of making itself large again even after it's been broken into a million pieces."

The one is a kind of warning that you need to measure your words and be careful of your behavior which wring a person's heart. The other is to promote awareness that whatever may happen, the human heart is not affected by the negative things depend on the owner's attitude. It is also underpinned by the truth that human being has a resilience and a natural healing power.

Your heart has a recovering method for itself.

40 USE THE POSITIVE LANGUAGE TO MAKE YOUR BRAIN WORK FOR YOU

*Words have energy and power with the ability to help, to heal,
to hinder, to hurt, to harm, to humiliate, and to humble.*

Yehuda Berg
Author and co-director of the Kabbalah Centre

An expert said that "Human brain has a characteristic that can't distinguish the positive from the negative." If you say, "Don't do @.", then the brain calls to mind @. As a result, it is the same response that you say, "Do @." The reason why you should say positive language in daily life.

Your brain governs the action, but it is a language that makes the brain work. The language you use is the expressions of your thoughts and your thoughts have a decisive effect on one's feelings and actions.

Feeling also influences the thoughts and action, and action affects the thoughts and feeling. A positive language can make your mental attitude positive. And a strong positive mental attitude will make miracles.

41 HAVE A PEACEFUL MIND, AND YOU WILL GET JUSTICE

Justice does not come from the outside. It comes from inner peace.

Barbara Hall
American television writer

There is a saying that "Everything depends on the mind." It's true. The mind makes up everything. You only see what you want to see. In Buddhism, existence itself only what the mind creates. That is, the existence of a word, concept, or thing is the expression of the mind. It depends on the individual mind whether it stands to sense, and it tells right from wrong.

When you call justice, it comes from not external factors but inner peace. Have a peaceful mind!

42 PLEASE TALK KIND WORDS, WHICH ECHO ARE GREAT

Kind words can be short, and easy to speak,
but their echoes are truly endless.

Mother Theresa

When you cross the Mapo Bridge over the Han River in Seoul, Korea, you can see lots of slogans or quotes on the rail of the bridge. They are made up of the passages or famous quotes that intend to stop the people who came to the bridge thinking about giving up their life.

Some slogans or quotes are very serious, others are very funny and humorous. It is true the words of the passages will save their lives. Regardless of the exact words of the passages, kind words with love can move the people's minds who read or listen to the slogans or quotes.

I am certain that when a person who is saved his/her life thanks to a kind word, the pleasant aftertaste will be remembered endless. From the speakers' view, the kind words might be easy to say, and they can take lightly. However, they are very priceless and give readers or listeners the courage and hope. Words can hurt or heal the mind.

A kind word to someone might save his/her life. Please talk kind words, which echo are great in daily life. The echoes of kind words are never-ending.

43 WHEN ONE DOOR CLOSES,
SEE THE OTHER DOOR OPENED

When one door closes, another opens;
but we often look so long and so regretfully upon the closed door that
we do not see the one which has opened for us.

Alexander Graham Bell
Scottish-born American inventor, scientist, and engineer

Have you ever felt you were blocked in a closet where there is no door or window? I have experienced that. If so, how did you get over that moment?

I got over it from a counsel with a pastor. He gave me a piece of good advice and I felt comfort and recovery hope. Thanks to his comfort and encouragement, I am here now. He said to me, "If you get lost in a maze, there must be an exit. When you were blocked in a closet, you got there because there was an entrance. So, there is also a way out."

When I am so embarrassed about the human relations that I wish I could crawl under a rock, he encouraged me that "I know your life. you had better become brazen about your business or human relations." His advice made me in pain to their spirit and I felt light of heart.

Do you feel pressure on your chest? Take a deep breath. And look up in the sky.

Do you feel you were blocked in a closet? Don't watch the door that closed already. Turn your eyesight on the other side of the closet. Then you can find a dim light somewhere. The light leads you to the other door open. When one door closes, another opens. Look around with open eyes.

No one can close you in a closet with no door or windows.

44 LIVE YOUR PRESENT FULLY

We do not heal the past by dwelling there;
we heal the past by living fully in the present.

Anonymous

Many people do not enjoy their present, because of being tormented by the past. It is miserable if you don't enjoy your present being chained to the past. Unfortunately, there are so many people around us that they do not enjoy due to the past. The past is only the past. By healing the past, you can enjoy your lives fully. And the only way to heal your past is to live your present fully.

Make the situation your own. Try to use your time fully. And you will lead an affluent life.

45 KEEP YOUR BODY, MIND, AND SOUL A HARMONIOUS STATE

Health is a state of complete harmony of the body, mind and spirit.
When one is free from physical disabilities and mental distractions,
the gates of the soul open.

B.K.S. Iyengar
Founder of the style of yoga

Body and mind are one. Your thoughts have an influence on your feeling and action. A state of the body also affects your thoughts and mind. If you think of the positive things, you will feel better, your body is lighter and your action is also positive, too.

On the contrary, if you think of the negative things, you will feel bad, your body is getting worse and your action is also negative, too. If you say to be healthy, health is the state that not only the body but also mind and soul become harmonious. That is, health starts with positive thoughts. I hope you are healthy.

46 SOW THE SEEDS
OF GIVING, JOY, OR HAPPINESS

Be aware of the of seeds you are planting each day.
Seeds of giving, joy, and happiness will blossom into health, love, and prosperity.

J. J. Goldwag
Author of Creating a Healthy Divorce

The thoughts and words that you use in your daily lives are the same as planting seeds in the field of consciousness and subconsciousness like farmers plant seeds in the spring. Everyone hopes to stay healthy, loves someone, and wants to enjoy an opulent lifestyle.

However, many people are apt to nip off the leaves of health, love, and wealth with his/her momentary thoughts and words. Sowing the seeds is very important, but cultivating is also important. But sowing the seeds is the first thing you should do. It is said, "You reap what you sow, or an onion will not produce a rose."

Do you wish to be healthy, love, and rich? Sow the seeds of health, love, and rich the first.

47 LOVE YOURSELF
LIKE A COLORFUL RAINBOW

Dare to love yourself as if you were a rainbow with gold at both ends.

Aberjhani
A historian, columnist, and editor

There is no one like you in the world. You are so unique and dear. You are worthwhile to be loved and respected by itself. Love yourself. Accept yourself and be proud of yourself. To love yourself is the most important thing than any other thing. Loving yourself is the best method to cure or heal your body and mind if you have any scar.

Call your name every day. Caress your body and say, "I love you." "ooo, I love you."

48 MAKE YOURSELF HAPPY RIGHT NOW

Happiness does not depend upon who you are or what you have.
It depends solely upon what you think.

Dale Carnegie
American writer and lecturer

Everyone wants to be happy. So, their dream of happiness sacrifices the present, and after that, they would accomplish often more than ever before. People hope to get a better present than the past and to sweat for a better future than the present. I am also no exception. How about you?

Do your present appearance and what you have now made you happy? Of course, what you are and what you have can make you happy. If so, you are a happy person. But if you do not, you need to look at you for a moment. Perhaps it is not because of what you are or what you have, but because of your thoughts.

Determining whether you are happy or not may be due to the different standards of happiness in your mind, rather than your appearance or your wealth. Happiness varies from moment to moment depending on what you think. Get the moment to choose happiness.

49 SEE HOPE THROUGH THE HURT HOLE IN THE MIND

Hope is being able to see that there is light despite all of the darkness.

Desmond Tutu
South African Anglican cleric and theologian

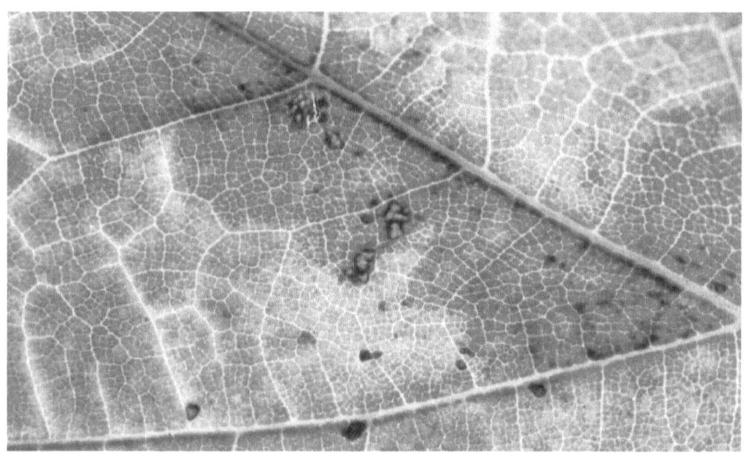

A few years ago, I visited one of my juniors who runs a business for a meeting as a consultancy and after the meeting, we had lunch together. It was a large restaurant in the complex mall with a large clothing store. When I sat down, I found a wonderful poem written on the table paper. I read the poem again and again and I was moved deeply. And I could hardly say anything for a while.

The title was "Leaves with holes gnawed by insects by Saeng-Jin Lee, a Korean poet." There were many similarities at that time between the life of my junior and mine also the same as the insects-eaten leaves. Hurt and hearted broken... However, my junior has been growing a lot in business. When I took a picture of the poem with my smartphone because I liked the poem on the first pitch, my junior said he also carried the poem on his smartphone. We smiled at each other. Because we knew each other's hurt without saying anything. And seeing the hope through that small hole...

The poet says that the leaves are pretty because they were eaten by insects. There is a bug hole in the oak leaf. So, the leaf is pretty because we can see the blue sky through the hole. The poet says that the leaves are pretty because they were eaten by insects. There is a big bug hole in the oak leaf. He also says the leaf is pretty because we can see the blue sky through the hole. He added, "I know it's wrong to say to be pretty because leaves have a hole. However, the trace of living by feeding others is as beautiful as a star."

50 ACCEPT MISERABLE FEELING AS A POSITIVE SIGNAL OF BRINGING YOU GOOD NEWS

*The only way to avoid being miserable is not to have enough leisure
to wonder whether you are happy or not.*

George Bernard Shaw
Irish playwright

I don't like the word 'miserable.' Because if I feel miserable, it means I am very unhappy with a certain situation. However, I cannot avoid having the time to be felt miserable.

What do you do if you feel miserable?

When you feel miserable, accept it as a positive signal that will bring you good news soon.

I am trying to accept the moment as a positive signal that gives me a chance to escape worse thing that would happen to me soon.

51 USE HYPNOTIC SUGGESTIONS TO HELP YOURSELF

If you say to yourself 'It's difficult to get up in the morning',
'It's hard to cease smoking', then you are
already using hypnotic suggestions on yourself....

Richard Bandler
Co-creator of the Neuro-linguistic programming

There is a proverb in Korea that "A word may repay a thousand dollar worth of debts." Its meaning is the same as "A soft answer turns away wrath," "Good words are good cheap," or "Good words cost nought." It's a good example of how important words between people is during communication.

Can you move the others' minds with words you talk to?

The words you talk to yourself in your daily life play a more important role in your life than the words you talk to others. The words you talk to yourself, that is your self-talk governs your act or what you do.

Your brain tends to be trying to achieve things as soon as you are thinking and talking about it. What you are thinking or what you are talking about is someday getting to have results. What you said to yourself is to become a hypnotic suggestion in your unconsciousness. And then your subconscious mind is trying to come what you said to reality. Even now, you are reading this book, you might be also thinking or have self-talk something.

Use hypnotic suggestions to improve your life, to cure your body, and heal your mind.

52 MAKE YOUR LIFE DYNAMIC OR COLORFUL

Life is like a cup of tea. It's all in how you make it.

Irish Proverb

What are you seeing at present?
What are you hearing now?

If your life has a color, what color do you want to be seen?
If your life is a kind of food, what food do you want to be cooked?

As Irish proverb saying, life is like a cup of tea. And the taste or aroma of the tea depends on how you make it. Just as the taste of tea at the tip of the tongue and the aroma of stimulating the nose depend on the amount of the water and temperature, so does your life is the same as.

What kind of life do you want to make?

Only you can make your life colorful or dull, dynamic or monotonous, and positive or negative. It is only you that can choose to be a leader or to be a follower.

ABOUT THE AUTHOR

Andrew Yoo, Ph.D. is an NLP Trainer and Consultant who is a member of the Global Training & Consulting Community of NLP University founded by Robert Dilts, Santa Cruz, the USA since 2005. Also, a participant of "Jack Canfield's Breakthrough to Success – Las Vegas August 2005."

At present, he is the CEO and Producer of Trans4mind Korea, the Personal Development Training Center for Korean Language Users all over the World. Trans4mind is a well-known brand in the field of Personal Development Training and a Global Network founded and run by Peter Shepherd and Wallace Huey that offers a wealth of free Personal Development Resources, Training, and Coaching.

He was once an English teacher at high school, and a part-time lecturer at Inha University, Seoul Theological University, and Sungkyul University in Korea.

He also participated in various volunteer activities as a member of the Rotary International.

Dr. Yoo's philosophy and principles as an expert in the field of personal development as follows:

All human beings have their own excellence.
People have their own unique talents.
Everyone wants to have a better future than now.
People's lives depend on their own choice.
Everyone has resources that achieve what they want to.
The best way to predict the future is to create it.
People can only do what they believe they can do.
Dreams come true.

He expects the following through all his activities such as public speaking, writing, coaching, consulting, and training, etc.

To bring the people to the world of happiness and wellbeing.
To lead the people to find his/her purpose in life.
To encourage people to fulfill his/her spirituality.
To guide the people to share what he/she has now.
To help the people make his/her dreams come true.
To lead the people to live his/her own lives.
To make the people strengthen his/her self-esteem and confidence.
To support the people to accept what he/she is and to appreciate it.

QUOTES FOR HEALING AND RECOVERY OF THE BODY AND MIND

1. *What happens when people open their hearts? They get better.*
   -Haruki Murakami

2. *The greatest healing therapy is friendship and love.* -Hubert H. Humphrey

3. *Having a low opinion of yourself is not "modesty". It's self-destruction. Holding your uniqueness in high regard is not "egotism". It's a necessary precondition to happiness and success.* -Bobbe Somme

4. *Just like there's always time for pain, there's always time for healing.*
   -Jennifer Brown

5. *You are free to choose your own way of life, but you are not free to choose the results.* -Herbert M. Shelton

6. *Gratitude is medicine for a heart devastated by tragedy. If you can only be thankful for the blue sky, then do so.* -Richelle E. Goodrich

7. *The way you help heal the world is you start with your own family.*
   -Mother Teresa

8. *Love one another and help others to rise to the higher levels, simply by pouring out love. Love is infectious and the greatest healing energy.* -Sai Baba

9. *Of one thing I am certain, the body is not the measure of healing, peace is the measure.* -Phyllis McGinley

10. *Music is such a great healing balm and a great way to forget your troubles.* -Ricky Skaggs

11. *The words of kindness are more healing to a drooping heart than balm or honey.* -Sarah Fielding

12. *The secret of health for both mind and body is not to mourn for the past, not to worry about the future, or not to anticipate troubles, but to live the present moment wisely and earnestly.* -Buddha

13. *A strong positive attitude will create more miracles than any wonder drug.* -Patricia Neal

14. *It is health that is real wealth and not pieces of gold and silver.* -Mahatma Gandhi

15. *Our bodies communicate to us clearly and specifically if we are willing to listen.* -Shakti Gawain

16. *Everyone has a doctor in him or her; we just have to help it in its work. The natural healing force within each one of us is the greatest force in getting well.* -Hippocrates

17. *Never hurry. Take plenty of exercise. Always be cheerful. Take all the sleep you need. Expect to be well.* -James Freeman Clarke

18. *All healing Starts in the mind.* -Alison Stormwolf

19. *True enjoyment comes from activity of the mind and exercise of the body; the two are ever united.* -Humboldt

20. *I have seen what a laugh can do. It can transform almost unbearable tears into something bearable, even hopeful.* -Bob Hope

21. *Learn to deal with the fact that you are not a perfect person, but you are a person that deserves respect and honesty.* -Pandora Poikilos

22. *The power of imagination makes us infinite.* -John Muir

23. *Gracious words are a honeycomb, sweet to the soul and healing to the bones.* -Proverbs 16:24(NIV)

24. *There are only two ways to live your life. One is as though nothing is a miracle. The other is as though everything is a miracle.* -Albert Einstein

25. *Medicine is only palliative. For behind disease lies the cause and this cause NO DRUG can reach.* -Dr. Weir Mitchell MD

26. *Don't find fault. Find a remedy.* - Henry Ford

27. *I love sharing my story. It's endlessly healing.* -Ben Vereen

28. *Where humanity sowed faith, hope, and unity, joy's garden blossomed.* -Aberjhani

29. *I cannot do all the good that the world needs, but the world needs all the good that I can do.* -Jana Stanfield

30. *A broken bone can heal, but the wound a word opens can fester forever.* -Jessamyn West

31. *There are so many ways to heal. Arrogance may have a place in technology, but not in healing. I need to get out of my own way if I am to heal.* -Anne Wilson Schaef

32. *Healing is a matter of time, but it is sometimes also a matter of opportunity.* -Hippocrates

33. *The soul is healed by being with children.* -Fyodor Dostoevsky

34. *Healing takes courage, and we all have courage, even if we have to dig a little to find it.* -Tori Amos

35. *If you want to be different, do something different.* -Wynton Marsalis

36. *There is no remedy for love but to love more.* -Henry David Thoreau

37. *Our sorrows and wounds are healed only when we touch them with compassion.* -Buddha

38. *Don't hold to anger, hurt, or pain. They steal your energy and keep you from love.* -Leo Buscaglia

39. *The human heart has a way of making itself large again even after it's been broken into a million pieces.* -Robert James Waller

40. *Words have energy and power with the ability to help, to heal, to hinder, to hurt, to harm, to humiliate, and to humble.* - Yehuda Berg

41. *Justice does not come from the outside. It comes from inner peace.* -Barbara Hall

42. *Kind words can be short, and easy to speak, but their echoes are truly endless.* -Mother Theresa

43. *When one door closes, another opens; but we often look so long and so regretfully upon the closed door that we do not see the one which has opened for us.* -Alexander Graham Bell

44. *We do not heal the past by dwelling there; we heal the past by living fully in the present.* -Anonymous

45. *Health is a state of complete harmony of the body, mind and spirit. When one is free from physical disabilities and mental distractions, the gates of the soul open.* -B.K.S. Iyengar

46. *Be aware of the of seeds you are planting each day. Seeds of giving, joy, and happiness will blossom into health, love, and prosperity.* -J. J. Goldwag

47. *Dare to love yourself as if you were a rainbow with gold at both ends.* -Aberjhani

48. *Happiness does not depend upon who you are or what you have. It depends solely upon what you think.* -Dale Carnegie

49. *Hope is being able to see that there is light despite all of the darkness.* -Desmond Tutu

50. *The only way to avoid being miserable is not to have enough leisure to wonder whether you are happy or not.* -George Bernard Shaw

51. *If you say to yourself 'It's difficult to get up in the morning', 'It's hard to cease smoking', then you are already using hypnotic suggestions on yourself....* -Richard Bandler

52. *Life is like a cup of tea. It's all in how you make it.* -Irish Proverb